"*People You Know, Places You've Been* brings 'little signs of magic in such / an un-whimsical world.' In this collection of poetry and visual art, hazy telephone poles against sky-rise buildings are a sight of beauty, a diner down the road has the best breakfast, and a subway commute is a scene from a movie. You are the main character in a world full of encounters with antiheroes, supporting characters, and nemeses. From aunties to teenage couples in vacation towns to hot professors, each moment makes life more alive. Shafi's words guide us to 'romanticize your ugly life' and to 'think of small blessings / as grand gestures.' In this collection, and the world Shafi creates, 'loving you is so wonderfully easy.'"
—Manahil Bandukwala, author of *MONUMENT*

"*People You Know, Places You've Been* is a touching and engaging collection of everyday moments and connections seen through the viewfinder of Hana Shafi's glorious and immensely creative mind. A joy to read."
—Farzana Doctor, author of *You Still Look the Same*

"*People You Know, Places You've Been* is a spellbinding collection of poems and drawings that thoughtfully describes the discomfort and beauty of everyday life. Shafi skillfully pairs humour and tenderness to depict familiar people and places through a lens of nostalgia, rage, and feminist thought."
—Ambivalently Yours, author of *Fire and Other Feelings*

Praise for
Small, Broke, and Kind of Dirty:
Affirmations for the Real World

"Narratives like Shafi's are ones I wished I had at a younger age but am ever grateful for now. This is why the stories of marginalized voices hold the utmost importance. Not only does the author deserve to take up space but also the impact it has on other marginalized people reading these narratives is monumental. Thank you, Hana Shafi, for being our Dolly Parton—in the way you know in your heart that she will accept you wholeheartedly, thank you for the belief that you will accept us as we are, too."
—*Canthius*

"If a summer feel-good movie was a collection of sweet affirmations, this would be it. Touching, honest, and everything I wish I had read growing up as an awkward kid."
—Anasimone George, comedian

"Shafi's loving affirmations alongside her storytelling and visual art make for the perfect rainy day read with a cup of chai."
—*Hamilton Review of Books*

"Hana Shafi writes important, intelligent, and honest essays that encourage understanding, essential thinking, create dialogue, and are a channel for tenderness."
—Bif Naked, singer and songwriter

"With her brash wit and honesty on display, this is the book that Frizz Kid / Hana Shafi fans (and new fans) have been waiting for."
—Vivek Shraya, author of *The Subtweet* and *I'm Afraid of Men*

Praise for
It Begins With The Body

"This book is the anthem of my youth."
—Alysha Brilla, Juno Award-nominated musician and songwriter

"Hana Shafi writes with a powerful and devastating honesty
about the things women are told they ought not talk about. From
body hair and financial angst to heartbreak and self-doubt, Shafi
examines all the expectations society places on women—and pushes
back against these outrages with a voice that is both vulnerable and
damning. A brilliant and incisive book, full of rage and love in all the
places where you need it to be."
—Lauren McKeon, author of *F-Bomb, Dispatches from the War
    on Feminism*

"Hana Shafi's work is a sigh of relief for the queer Muslim brown kid
I was, and the queer Muslim brown adult I now am. It's the act of
visibility, of being seen through the words on a page that are so life
affirming. I feel grateful that I'm of a time where art like this is being
made. It's relatable, it's a delight."
—Fariha Róisín, co-host of *Two Brown Girls* podcast

PEOPLE You KNOW, PLaCeS you've BEEN

poems and
illustrations

Hana Shafi

PEOPLE YOU KNOW, PLACES YOU'VE BEEN

poems and
illustrations

Hana Shafi

Book*hug Press
Toronto 2023

Title: People you know, places you've been : poems and illustrations / Hana Shafi.
Names: Shafi, Hana, 1993- author, illustrator.
Identifiers: Canadiana (print) 20230221270 | Canadiana (ebook) 20230221289
   ISBN 9781771668538 (softcover)
   ISBN 9781771668545 (EPUB)
   ISBN 9781771668552 (PDF)
Subjects: LCGFT: Poetry.
Classification: LCC PS8637.H345 P46 2023 | DDC C811/.6—dc23

The production of this book was made possible through the generous assistance of the Canada Council for the Arts and the Ontario Arts Council. Book*hug Press also acknowledges the support of the Government of Canada through the Canada Book Fund and the Government of Ontario through the Ontario Book Publishing Tax Credit and the Ontario Book Fund.

Book*hug Press acknowledges that the land on which we operate is the traditional territory of many nations, including the Mississaugas of the Credit, the Anishnabeg, the Chippewa, the Haudenosaunee and the Wendat peoples. We recognize the enduring presence of many diverse First Nations, Inuit and Métis peoples and are grateful for the opportunity to meet and work on this land.

Book*hug Press

It was but yesterday I thought myself a fragment quivering without rhythm in the sphere of life.
Now I know that I am the sphere, and all life in rhythmic fragments moves within me.
—Kahlil Gibran

Contents

Chapter 1: Antiheroes 9

apple pie 10
tough teen bitches 13
heroines 14
good trash 16
Chatty Cathy 19

lucid 21
off-white knight 23
suburban doors 24
hero 26

Chapter 2: Supporting Characters 29

pink 30
the four horsemen 32
god bless america
    and white dad 34
the friends 35

kids say the darnedest things 36
the kids pt. 2 38
never have i ever 39
loving you 42

Chapter 3: Palaces 43

don't cry over late breakfast 44
the antique store 46
one man's trash 49
gated communities 50

vacation town 52
antidotes to my wretched
    existence 55

Chapter 4: Nemesis 57

occupation: musician 58
cookies and gold stars for
    your support 60
beware of the rogue auntie 62
bang 64

triumph over villainess at
    the farmers market 65
the edgy male decrees 66
wolves 69

Chapter 5: Dungeons 71

public transit should be free 72
places of higher learning 75
blank room 77

public transit should be free;
   the epilogue 79
don't feed the birds 82
bad taste great life 84

Chapter 6: Beautiful Leading Role 87

the halo effect 88
laundry queen 93
all money is always dirty 95

hot professor 96
the pink lady 98
rules for everyone 100

Chapter 7: Liminal Spaces 101

gasoline 102
law and order: check-out
   counter 104
mall rats 106

waiting room at the edge
   of the cosmos 108
the salon 110
that one house 112
the street you grew up on 115

Chapter 8: Wizards and Crones 117

the collector 119
everybody ages 120
the dichotomy of grannies 122

poet 124
a nana like mine 125

Acknowlegements 129

About the Author 131

Chapter 1:
Antiheroes

noun: **antihero**
a central character in a story, movie, or drama
who lacks conventional heroic attributes

apple pie

when my friend leaves, they say
he's regrouping
"regrouping."
i think that's because alcohol scatters people

i imagine
if he was a million pieces
thrown upon the sidewalk
he'd be coins, and multicoloured jelly beans,
and bottle caps, and pencils,
and teeth, and copper,
and those random pieces of
gravel or sand
that somehow end up in all old pockets

a lot of alcoholics are like that
scattered
there's one at the local bar
those pre-plague times
when he didn't see me for a month
he'd say it's been a year
i tell him it's not the case
then acquiesce
"yes, it's been a year,"
i figure his memories are scattered
and they are
as bright as they are blurry,
and friendly, and kind,
and hopeful,
and lost too

my friend left with me
our unfinished art project
his pencil remained
it needs my ink

friend, i will finish your drawing
while you pick up
the scattered things on the sidewalk
worn and lovely,
grimy and gleaming,
and tuck them back into yourself
beneath familiar skin
where all scattered things go

tough teen bitches

she was the scariest girl in school
suspended a number of times
later expelled, hangs in the toughest
of crowds, i heard she ripped out
a chunk of some girl's hair, i heard
she draws blood when she fights
she's the real deal, and damn you
alphabetical seating arrangement
we were desk buddies in English

every day i sat tensely, forced myself
to sit quietly, don't wheeze, breathe
sometimes my nose whistles
but i put a stop to that.

doodling during class, she looks
at my notebook
"is that *Lord of the Rings*?" she asks
"um, ya," oh no, what if she punches people
who watch *Lord of the Rings*?
"i love those movies!
i watched them all during christmas break!"
her smile is warm and i figure
she's not so scary after all

heroines

"you're too hot to have a stain on your shirt"
she hauls my big sister to the sink
grabs her shirt and scrubs,
a hefty glob of that neon-pink soap
ever abundant in public bathrooms

she yanks her to the dryer
stretches the fabric,
manically waves her hand
to keep the automatic going
"all done!" we erupt in a chorus
of thank yous as she
smiles and saunters away
a total stranger, mind you,
offering spontaneous laundry service
to a girl in need

she just came in here to pee
not prepared for stained polyester
but women will be heroines if they must
called to action in inopportune moments
especially in a public bathroom
cause she-warriors gotta shit too

good trash

dumpster divers are harmless
but they'll give you a fright at 3 a.m.
walking back to the apartment
through the back door, a head
pops up from the garbage void
you give that awkward flat smile
the one office workers exchange a lot
i call it "frog smile"
you give a frog smile and you're on your way

i've gotten things from the sidewalk
and the dump before
new furniture? in this economy?
but i've never actually been in one of those big containers
stupid prissy me,
i'm probably missing out on some good finds

the maintenance lady once climbed right in
found a pink purse, dusted it off
and took it to get the zipper fixed

my partner found a dirty mini fridge
the inside covered in mould, dirt, and
god knows what
diligently cleaned it
now he's dry-aging meat inside
a true success story

i think people call this area *sketchy*
because of the dumpster divers
plus the makeshift market just down the street
a crowd, considered unsavoury by some
sell old shoes, protein shakes,
adult diapers, tarnished DVDs,
and remarkably legit looking
fake gucci belts

if a lawyer in a nice suit
offers you coke
in some swanky place—the nice part of town—
there's nothing sketchy about that,
but dumpster divers who won't
take your money or fuck up your life
or leech off your misery
are the ones you worry
are lowering the property value

and if you think that, i feel bad for you
how pathetic that you don't know
the simple thrill
of finding some really good trash

Chatty Cathy

now,
we call him Big Guy
but i used to call him Chatty Cathy
absent for months
i turned to B and asked
"what if he's dead?"
"he's either off the streets or dead"

the ice thaws
Big Guy reappears
classic backwards baseball hat
he's not really allowed in the shop
on account of the loitering and rambling

he told me once that american girls are prettier
i asked him how he knows
"i just know"

we have a shared ritual
i tell him i can't talk because i'm working
he tells me if the store was gone,
i'd be out of a job and then
i could talk all the time
"that's true. but today i have a job"

when he leaves
i tell the customers
"he's all right, i know him"
in case a trigger-happy Karen
has a cellphone at the ready
unaware that he just wants to talk
and tell me that he likes wrestling
or that he doesn't like my sweater
and that if i didn't have a job
we could talk all the time

lucid

a hallucination-driven monologue
dissolves into lucidity
he apologizes profusely at 4 a.m.
the apparition in my window
that scares the bejesus out of me
"i forgot my keys."
i let him in, he says he didn't mean to scare me
and i believe him
a seemingly neurotypical interaction
among neighbours

mostly, he speaks of god
and in the beginning,
i thought he was a yuppie
with a bluetooth headset
topics vary
the family dynasty,
consorting with angels,
relations he won't approve of
sometimes anger,
sometimes sadness

he lights up by the window
and the world frets over what Zoom background to use
and how to organize a covert backyard gathering

i wonder if he's losing himself
i feel relieved to see him in the lobby still
pleased to know he speaks with god

what does isolation do
to the already alone?
the rhythm of his rant
a voice so determined,
quiet pauses of clarity
his silhouette in my window assuring me
the world cannot forget him

off-white knight

when the old lady falls boarding the bus
heavy bags in tow
he springs to her aid, white knight
lifts her up, checks her leg
just to be safe, grabs her bags
"i'm a paramedic, ma'am"
helps her grab a seat
sits back in peace

he's the only one on the bus not wearing a mask
he makes my principles itch
i need to hate him
but today i can't
tomorrow is another day

suburban doors

to me
the circumstances around your life
are still a mystery
as was your death

folks may say otherwise

i understand the preference
not to think about closed doors
and the quiet violence behind them
instability fenced in by stable lawns
and well-paved driveways

i have no choice but to think
it's always been this way
a devastating curiosity
to peer through walls and windows
screen doors and front porches
perfect landscaping and new roof work
all the way to the ugliness within

there is little to be sure of
what i know of you is incomplete
a frayed and uncertain timeline

but of three things i am certain:
one, that your smile was warm and reminded me of hazelnuts and
golden-hour light
two, that i do not believe in an afterlife and yet am sure there is a
peaceful one for you
and three, that most men don't deserve wives

hero

movies that tell us
people are better
movies with fairy tales
of well-dressed men and
fit women, just a small
handful who would risk it all
just for us average ugly folk
to keep living

we leave the stories
we look for
heroes in people
attractive doctors, feel-good headlines
like "second grader raises money
to pay for school lunches,"
(which is actually not feel-good at all)
we look for heroes in
good samaritans on the subway
don't worry about that guy going around
stabbing people with an X-Acto knife
some people are willing to give their seat up

little signs of magic in such
an un-whimsical world
we look for it in women's bathrooms
drunken confessions of how
beautiful we all are
you're beautiful girl
you look fantastic you're perfect
we're perfect this is the best night
a sentiment lost
in the following nauseous morning

hero worship creating
a slick transition to celebrity worship
famous actors
greeting terminal children
anonymous donors who turn out to be
grammy-winning pop stars
heroes in old organs
kickstarting new life
heroes in Gucci, heroes in
rags, rags to riches stories
heroes of the american dream

we are always looking
ever hopeful
tell ourselves
if it really came down to it
we could be heroes too

Chapter 2
Supporting Characters

adjective + noun: **supporting character**
a supporting character is a character in a narrative
that is not the focus of the primary storyline but is
important to the plot/protagonist

pink

we linger in the people we know
our faults are salt
upon watercolour
leave ripples, veins, and scars

our presence is blood
mixing into water
and now all the liquid in the glass
is pink

in all friends, lovers, and strangers,
ER nurses, distant family,
occasional acquaintances, peers,
teachers, waiters, online trolls,
baristas, bartenders, artists,
whoever sits across from you on the train
the person who got their drink before you
your best friend in the second grade
your worst enemy in the fifth grade
we all leave a little bleed
and they leave a little bleed in us too

there is no disconnecting
"us" from "them"
who we are now is only possible
because of anyone we've ever known
now, all the liquid is pink
all that we are mixes with everyone we were,
every place you've been
every person you know
swirls in the water so strangely
it becomes new matter
a thing entirely of its own

the four horsemen

the four horsemen are
the man who ghosted you after sex
the transit fare inspector
the girl from your hometown
(who is now waist-deep in a pyramid scheme)
and the friend who helped you give yourself bangs

god bless america and white dad

white dad chills in his garage
fixes car in his garage
watches the street
shakes his head
at the loud immigrants
moving in next door
white dad wears a polo
he's good with his kids
fixes a mean drink
loves his wife
wishes his wife
would shut the fuck up sometimes
white dad gives you shovelling pointers
you're not shovelling the snow right
only white dad knows
white dad likes to stare
keeps a cooler of beers
says stuff like
"nothing like a cold one on a hot day"
"better get out your snow tires"
"the grass is gonna love this"
white dad takes the family to disney world
buys a midlife-crisis convertible in
douchebag red
i have no idea how he can afford it
he's always just standing in that garage

the friends

two people hug in front of the farmers market
they stay in each other's embrace
longer than the appropriate amount
(which is 4 seconds if you didn't know)
they giggle and squeal in excitement,
the embrace growing
tighter, tougher over time
they block the entrance
they sway back and forth
their joy too obnoxious for some, but
for me, so deliciously all-encompassing
after all
why shouldn't all these miserable people stop for their joy?
why shouldn't we be inconvenienced
by a sudden spontaneous act of pure glee?
are we angry at this hug lasting for too long or
are we envious that we don't feel the way they do?
slowly, they come down from their ecstasy
and enter the market
their lingering happiness so potent
that all the fruit is sure to ripen sweetly

kids say the darnedest things

pretending a spoon is a knife
she bangs it on nothing
a make-believe meal
in the imaginary inn

"ok pretend you're 20 years old,
and ask for a room"
she orders.
scene 1, take 1, action.
"hi can i have a room."
excellent delivery,
the confidence of a 20-year-old
"yes, your room number is 206,
your activities are
dancing, singing, and art."

a plot twist, i didn't expect that
the scenario has changed
two seven-year-olds
running a hotel, a restaurant,
and an arts camp
all at once
look what late-stage capitalism has done

she leads her three steps
to a white chair
"ok this is your room."
i hope the rates are cheap

but before the plot really thickens,
mother calls the inn owner.
now i'll never know how the story ends

the kids pt. 2

today the scene is more focused
no more complicated all-in-one resorts
now it's just a restaurant
the children have delegated
there's a hostess, a waitress,
customers, and kitchen staff
they've even created a menu
dinner is "steak, salmon, rice"
dessert is Kit Kat
drinks are water, juice,
and piña colada, which, they've assured me,
is fake

"ok sit like a rich girl."
the set design is magnificent
a small table, real cutlery,
actual juice and chocolates
the scene is taking a dramatic turn
the rich girl customer is unruly
she complains of a chipped cup
she refuses a new cup and they discuss
a woman who had twins, but one died
and now i'm unsure of what's real
and what's pretend

the rich girl demands more Kit Kat
the kitchen staff are fighting
the waitress is getting flustered and
the hostess is being unhelpful
even in make-believe world,
restaurants are the toughest business to run

never have i ever

if you weren't a little traumatized
by your mean middle school gym teacher
we can't be friends
everyone's a little traumatized
by their mean middle school gym teacher
except athlete prodigies, and maybe even
still athlete prodigies

if you've never known a bad landlord
you were the landlord, and so
we can't be friends
if you call everyone that looks
just a little different than what you're used to
"sketchy"
we can't be friends
and it kind of sounds like you're
scared of poor people

if you like carbonated water
we can maybe be friends but
probably not,
because it tastes like liquid dust
if you've never cried so hard that your
heart was beating in your head
like really wailed and screamed
and sobbed so primally
like the toddler you once were
at least once
in your adult life
we can't be friends

if you've never listened to a guy
talk on and on about a creative project
that literally no one but him cares about
because it only exists to feed his own
stupendous ego,
we can't be friends and
you're very lucky
if you are that guy, seek help

if you've never loved someone so much
so ridiculously and they didn't love you back
and you really truly thought
you would never love so big
so bright and unceasing
again, but then a little time went on
and you were proved wrong
because of course
you can love again and honestly they
literally were not that great, relax
we can't be friends

if you've never been taken aback
by how scary the world is sometimes,
how meaninglessly violent we can be
unflinching in cruelty, overwhelmed by
multitudes of suffering
tragedy that is only offset by the vibrancy
of all our lived experiences, all the courage in when
we turn to face the sun and continue,
the sheer simple joy
in any small insignificant
moment in our complicated but pointless lives
we can't be friends

WE'RE ALL JUST ANIMALS SEARCHING FOR DOPAMINE

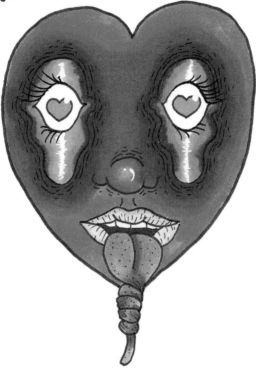

if you've really never looked up once
at wires and ugly cement buildings
and telephone poles silhouetted in an
orange and purple
pollution aesthetic
haze sunset and thought
well i guess
that really is beautiful
we will be friends once you see it

loving you

there are people i love who have moved on
and this is a beautiful thing
they've moved back to their hometowns
started to drink less
dropped out of school
left to mend themselves in private
and fix old pickup trucks
babysit their siblings
couch surf at their friends' homes
change programs and find new jobs
apply for ODSP
finally remembering to take their meds
finally remembering it's ok to call friends
becoming uncles and aunties
living with their parents again
living on their own again
reconciling with small upbringings
reconciling with big failures
i'm sad every day without them
and this is a beautiful thing
because i have loved so fully
and i continue while they're away
they have moved on and i am grateful
that there are things to move on to
that you can only let go when you have many things
and heal if you're so very alive
and to be alive is to have a body
and to have a body is human
missing someone is a privilege
and loving you is so wonderfully easy

Chapter 3
Palaces

noun: **palace**; plural noun: **palaces**
the official residence of a sovereign, archbishop,
bishop, or other exalted person

don't cry over late breakfast

the diner by the apartment has the best breakfast sausages
the grease-to-crispiness ratio is perfect
dylan is always trying to replicate them
every time has been delicious but not the same
he knows it's futile
sometimes the really good food is the bad food
and i can't explain why

one late breakfast at the diner
i saw a woman crying over her meal
as we left i asked if she was okay
"it looks like you're having a bad day"
"yes," she said, "a really bad day, but i'll be fine"

i wanted to believe that she would,
but she didn't order the breakfast sausages

the antique store

antique owners who are nice
have nothing of value
the older and more crotchety,
the better the goods

at the local spot,
she is always sitting
somewhat irritated
her helper
or husband
or hostage
whoever he is
wears one of those belts for heavy lifting
i suspect it's heavier than he is

madam—he calls her madam—
instructs him to lead me to the basement
i am a loyal customer after all
for a moment, i consider
my binge-watching of criminal minds
tomorrow's breaking news:
"two elderly antique shop owners murder local artist
her body found crammed
into a mahogany armoire circa 1951"
imagine, the value increase
on that piece of furniture

she is the dominant, the alpha,
it was her idea of course
he is her submissive, her lurch,
gets his hands dirty
wipes it out on the too-big belt
so hers can stay clean

i shrug and go anyway,
if this is the end, it's a good story
but it is not
he brings me boxes of gold frames,
caked in dust
"madam will know the prices"
indeed madam does,
i leave with three

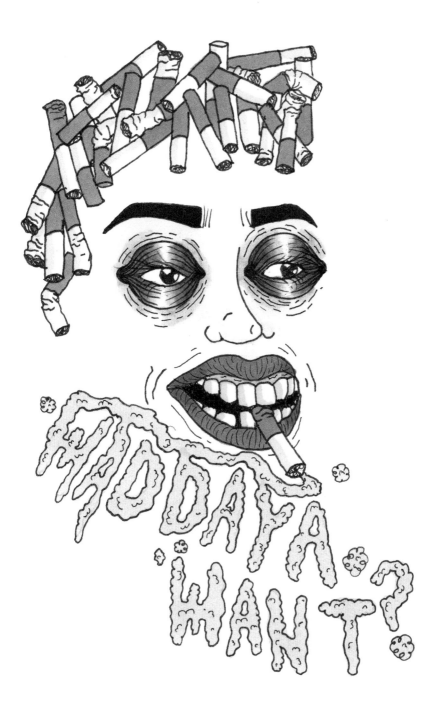

one man's trash

dylan's birthday trip is to value village
no matter what time of year you go
there will always be at least
one haunted doll,
one item engraved with a name and date
that no one but the previous owner could possibly find relevant
and several beer steins only for decorative purposes
there's always a lady there who smokes a lot
you smell her in the aisle
there's always an upper-class white woman
a visual artist in her 20s
striving to look semi-impoverished
there are, of course, the exhausted workers
most likely racialized and mothers
there's always a dad looking for khaki shorts.
and he's wearing khaki shorts he bought from there

i found a mini Mortal Kombat arcade machine,
tacky cowboy boots,
and a leopard-print skirt.
dylan found a cast iron pan,
a silver pot,
and a small TV that actually works

may your secondhand haul exceed your dreams

gated communities

i walk through the residential streets
of old toronto
to stare, unabashedly,
into the windows
admire the bookshelves, framed art,
flourishing houseplants, mounted TVs
and lazing pet(s)
residents coming into frame
white hair, white skin
beige granite in the kitchen

according to some wellness influencer online
if i think it, i will manifest it
capitalism cancels positive vibes
i know this
yet i walk here often
mantra in hand
keep thinking it keep thinking it
manifest harder, i wonder
if i peer in enough, will you let me in?
could i live this life with you?

i smile at the people walking their
purebred (meaning inbred) dogs
you cannot see my smile through my mask
and pull your french bulldog away
a sixth sense (wealth) alerting you
that a non-member is perusing the neighbourhood
there are no iron bars
but i know anyway
that i'm an intruder
in a gated community

so i walk back to my one-bedroom
my key always gets stuck in the
dreaded back door
keep thinking it, keep thinking it
a garbage picker gathers his finds and leaves
by the time the door finally opens
i'm on the ground floor, it's quick
now someone is peering through my window
at my always up christmas lights,
my purple couch, my two cats,
my dying air plant, my halloween snow globe
thinking will you let me in?
can i live this life with you?

vacation town

the teenage couple in the water
throw their bodies back and forth
he makes her laugh. i cannot help but watch
i know soon all will go downhill
it's not cruel it's just inevitable

if they are here on vacation
he will break her heart during the school year
if they are locals
he may break her heart only after
he gets her pregnant
it's not rude to assume it's just inevitable

their metabolisms will slow
he'll get a beer belly
she'll get hips so wide
she'll struggle to find the right jeans
since women's jeans are never made
with women's bodies in mind
it's not fair but it's inevitable

today they gleam and i am
gleaming too,
out in the water
where life has no consequence
the wave pulls and we push against it
and the dance feels good

though it's just a vacation
and it's just another beach
and it's just another august
like all augusts before and
all augusts after
it all feels perfect today
and that, too,
is inevitable

antidotes to my wretched existence

snack on wild tomatoes at the park
and go to a karaoke bar alone and sober
enter a cemetery after dark
smoke on a bench and
smile at your neighbour even if
you think (and know) they're a weirdo
wear a beautiful dress
just to run errands,
you won't get another chance to wear it
write in a leather-bound notebook
to make the words seem more important
watch a cat sunbathe,
pet at your own discretion,
interpret a monarch butterfly as a prophetic message
find symbols in unremarkable things
see sunlight through a tree canopy
interpret it as angelic

drink cheap tea out of expensive china
draw a person on the subway
badly even, though refrain
from making eye contact
listen to movie soundtracks while you commute
pretend to be a mysterious stranger
by wearing an odd hat,
stop someone just to say
"i like your shoes"
sit in places of worship
different from your own faith
then talk to someone else's god

romanticize your ugly life,
not as frivolous daydream but to
stop your soul from slow erosion,
don't avoid life's terrible questions
answer instead with confidence
that we have to think of small blessings
as grand gestures
and grand failures as small lessons
experience life as a novel
instead of a slow receipt
adding up until we die

pretend a small town could be paris
walk to the corner store
to buy iced tea and an epiphany
nod to a stranger
while in the throes of a misanthropic episode

and if it's hard and if it feels forced
if it feels trite and saccharine
and exhausting
if people and places and their problems
and your baggage
have worn you down
for the last
fucking
time
then start small
and snack on some wild tomatoes
in the park

Chapter 4
Nemesis

noun: **nemesis**; plural noun: **nemeses**
a long-standing rival; an archenemy

occupation: musician

there are skinny boys who play guitar
it's not my thing
but it used to be
when i was 21 and hated myself.

when you hate yourself you may find yourself
dating a bass player
"what do you do?"
"i'm a bass player."
"wow. he's a bass player."

his band's music is terrible
it's not that you lie when you say
"your music is awesome,"
it's just that when you have low self-esteem,
and you're gaining weight,
and you're 21, and possibly (probably)
underemployed
and the cyst growing under your cheek is hard to cover with foundation

this music really does sound good

you won't snap out of it and break up with him
he'll ghost you
and when you grow
and you realize bodies change
and dreams will change and it won't always
be this way
and you realize a hot compress on a cyst is better than foundation
then you'll realize
his music was never very good

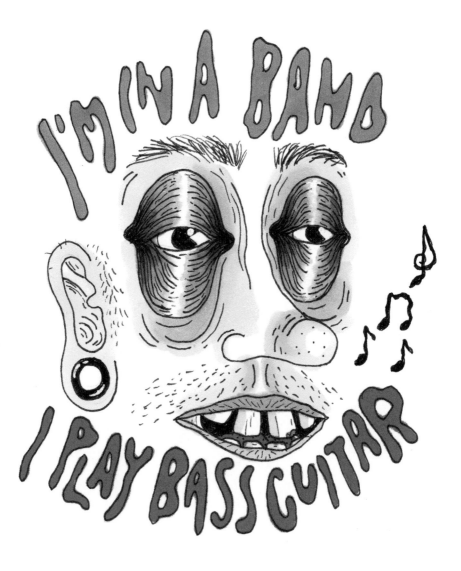

cookies and gold stars for your support

there's probably a bartender
or bassist or photographer or something
somewhere in the city
tall, has a great haircut
wears a tank top that says
feminist or girl power or whatever
he figures, this makes him a good ally
but that's not being an ally

and he gives free JD shots to pretty women
he figures, this makes him a good ally
but that's not being an ally

he changes the banner of his profile picture
on women's day
but that's not being an ally

he tells you he thinks
you're beautiful
even though you don't shave your pits
but that's not being an ally

he says he gets turned on
by *all women*
but that's not being an ally

he goes to indie punk shows time to time
but that's not being an ally
he says
that you're brave or whatever for being
a woman but
that's not being an ally
and he and he and he
is nice to lots of women but
hangs out with known creeps but
doesn't really mean it but
takes "edgy" photographs of white women but
never donated to your cause but

it's okay 'cause he bought the tank top
and that's not being an ally

beware of the rogue auntie

this auntie prowls the neighbourhood
she is a lioness
hunting grounds include weddings and dinner parties
scours to feed her family, yes, but
mostly to bloat her own ego
her children will all be doctors or engineers
your children will never outshine them
they will marry into the best families
yours will remain degenerate spinsters
or controversial elopers
over tea she whips up the latest tale
success and prosperity is in her home
are you jealous? you should be

it is not in your home
she lies all the time
aaaaaall the time
so much that
i question if she's honest even with god

in her hubris, she believes
even an omnipotent being
could fall for a confidently pitched
PR spin.
auntie is a contradiction
she's wearing grandma's dressing gown
but her teeth are so big, so sharp,
she is a pious socialite
the pastel domestic knife of Abraham
call her on her bluff, i dare you
but you won't
once auntie gets going
the rest of us are just lambs

bang

he sits outside the window in his walker
pretends to shoot squirrels with a cap gun
"bang, you're dead"
he laughs, reloads, keeps going
says people aren't like they used to be
says he's 65
or 75 or 85 i can't remember
over the sound of plastic caps
he hums a tune
engages with the occasional tenant
too polite to ignore an elderly man
with a strange hobby
"all out, no bullets left" he chuckles
i breathe easy now
his old eccentricities make me nervous
the pop of the plastic gun makes my cats nervous
the constant threat of death,
though fake,
makes the squirrels nervous
they think he's a harmless old gent
he probably is
but i worry he may be a bastard
who's always liked making people nervous

triumph over villainess at the farmers market

i took your squash, martha
i took your squash
we both saw the same perfectly patterned squash
at the farmers market
and i got it first
and you went to take it, yes you did
and the man said "sorry she just bought that one"
and i saw the life leave your eyes, barbara
because i took your squash
hahahahahaha
you would've cooked it into a hearty fall stew
or used it to decorate your mantelpiece
above your beautiful fireplace but now
it will rot on my table
in my disgusting rented apartment
and my cats will mar its perfect patterns by
attempting to bite it because they are idiots
and it's so sweet because i won
because good always triumphs over evil
the good guys win
because
i
took
your
squash

the edgy male decrees

"so have you seen *Bloodsport*?"
"well I'm wearing the shirt aren't i?"
ladies beware, lest ye be judged
by an edgy male who surely knows
more about pop culture than you do.
they are many! they are legion!
they rain down in hordes
"do you even like this band?
name one album!"
quickly, now, if you hesitate
he will strike! he'll call you fake.
fake nerd. fake gamer.
fake bitch. Lo, they will reveal you
as a false god.
"which Batman comic is your favourite?"
"have you even read the book?"
"do you know any *Star Wars* expanded universe lore?"
"those are singles. you don't even know deep tracks."
we are weary from battle,
there are too many, save yourself!
dare not leave the house in your
favourite tee, for the enemy is waiting

wolves

there's one in every family
not a black sheep, no
much worse
the domestically violent fanatic
the remorseless liar
the walking white-collar crime
the literal rapist
the possible skinhead
the pious devil
the rage-aholic time bomb
the relentless taker
and somehow they are
always there
perhaps, in your family,
they've been excommunicated;
in most families they walk amongst us
we know they have teeth
we know they are hungry
but the family says close your eyes
look away
if they bite you, wince quietly
if you bleed, it's OK
they may be a wolf
but they're family
and blood is thicker than water

Chapter 5
Dungeons

noun: **dungeon**; plural noun: **dungeons**
a strong underground prison cell, especially in a
castle

public transit should be free

like most good ol'-fashioned
red-blooded workers
i have my most toxic thoughts
on public transit
off of it, i am ready
to fight in the class war
on it, i wish only to ascend
to the upper echelons—people who hire drivers

if you've been on public transit
you can't judge me, for you've thought
what i've thought
these people are disgusting
who stinks
this city is filled with degenerates
if this subway doesn't move i'll kill myself
if this asshole doesn't move i'll kill him too
i'm gonna stab this manspreader in the dick
turn your shitty music off
look at this piece of shit
i hate you all

and then it happens
a dog trots on
you stare into its big eyes
not a single thought behind them
just a happy animal
and the owner lovingly pats the dog
on its little head
says "good dog"
and the anger melts away
maybe people aren't so bad

but the dog leaves
and i get back to dreaming of violence

places of higher learning

the campus, tote bags, textbook receipts
coffee and brown shoes
you played beer pong
put some dead celebrity's poster
in your dorm room
we sunk, ran out of
time and sleep
you wore the school colours
waved flags at homecoming
we lingered between class
worked odd jobs
you went to themed parties
we caught the bus back to our parents
you graduated with honours
pieced memories together
on a corkboard collage
we graduated too tired to care
done tearing ourselves apart
the campus is your beginning
the campus is our end
the campus is a school
the campus is a graveyard
the campus built you up
the campus broke us down
but the campus cost you
the campus cost us too
and we both still drink coffee
we both wear brown shoes

blank room

adult cis het men have a tendency
to live in blank rooms
you've been in this room before
the bed—if there is, in fact
a bed per se—is not made,
there's clothes on the floor
and the walls
the walls are just blank

there are no photos, posters, or frames
no knickknacks or tchotchkes
no plants no discernible
signs of a personality
but he has a personality
one that you are currently pretending is a good personality
but it's not
it's quite awful

now, it's not blankness as a style
it's not minimalism
it's not zen
the blankness is not premeditated
it's just
some type of lazy masculinity
and some of you might say
no no that's not true
you're a fool, search your memory
you've been in this room before
this half-dirty half-clean room
this room without traces of sentimentality
this room devoid of nostalgia

or any hints of emotional maturity
this room that only exists
for sleeping and jerking off
and now you're in it and all you can think is
damn boy you live like this?

and i think, against your better judgment
you may have stayed in that room
if your glasses were rosier than usual
you maybe even tried to spruce it up
i think, maybe, you even
gave him art, or bought him a plant
or tried to leave something of yours behind
you tried to breathe life into his blank room
took the toxic traits of his personality
to clumsily morph them into something
that could pass for eccentric,
stoic or quirky
but you failed, and it's not your fault,
you will always fail at this
so will she who comes after you
you can't save his blank room
go back home to yours

public transit should be free; the epilogue

he's facedown on a seat in the streetcar
"is he... y'know?"
my friend turns around
"i don't know. maybe."
a few minutes go by, he wakes up
"he's not dead," i say
"that's good," they reply

are we so used
to the slow, casual death
of the city's poorest
that it hardly stirs a feeling?
or is this a sick evolutionary necessity?
turn off feelings
say nothing
get through commute

if he was dead
how long would it have taken for anyone to notice?
it likely would've taken a fare inspector
to see if he paid for the ride
nudge him gingerly
more concerned that he didn't pay
than the fact that he's facedown
sleeping in a streetcar because he has no home

and everyone,
in the interest of self-preservation,
tries not to notice the withering
tries to pay their fare
and get on with the day
and hopes that the streetcar home
has less dead people

don't feed the birds

the hungriest neighbourhoods
have the most well-fed pigeons
among the poor,
a few elderly ambassadors are chosen
they choose themselves
or maybe god does
throwing seed dutifully, diligently
day in
day out
sitting among
that chaotic cooing
perhaps they are kindred spirits
knowing what it's like to congregate and live
so crowded and frenzied

we, too, could be a dirty nuisance
we, too, are plenty and overwhelming
and ultimately innocent
in privileged streets,
the signs are erected
"don't feed the birds"

bad taste great life

i suspect their neighbours think the lights are tacky
in a historic neighbourhood
lawn lights illuminate the house
from green to blue
purple to pink
red to yellow
and back 'round again
but i like to see the proof
that someone fun lives inside

the windows of the other homes
reveal interiors that look like schematics
minimalist decor, stark white,
rail-thin lamp mirroring rail-thin wife,
strategically placed vase
with a few strands of dyed pampas

one large painting above couch
abstract and unyielding though
likely not an original
something leather
something marble
open space throughout
sterile colour palette
so i doubt they cook with turmeric

the richer you become,
the fewer things you have
my one-bedroom is covered
in treasured cheap crap and stickers
a dead giveaway to my low income, surely
such tackiness would not be acceptable
in the affluent boroughs
(unless that tackiness comes in the form of bespoke furniture)

on the bench, during my nighttime lurk
i watch old victorian trim glow in technicolor
mesmerized by
the changing lights
a positive indicator
that even the unstylish and less refined
could own a nice home

Chapter 6
Beautiful Leading Role

adjective + adjective + noun: **beautiful leading role**
a leading actor, leading actress, star, or simply lead,
plays the role of the protagonist of a film or play

the halo effect

the man across from me at the coffee shop
is a perfect man,
by arbitrary standards yes, but
we live in an arbitrary society so
the conclusion is the same:
he is a perfect man
a cross between hercules
and marlon brando
and maybe one of those straights
who make bank in gay-for-pay porn;
with a face like that, why not?

he wears a white shirt
like he invented white shirts
how does the world turn for him?
what bad thing really happens
to a man who looks like that?
the type of man whose face
never cracked under the weight of bad news
because bad news could not touch
such pretty skin

i imagine
he enters his workplace
while coworkers throw rose petals at his feet
he sees the world with brighter colours
the flowers smell more sweet
the fruit is dripping with juices

if i was very beautiful,
i don't think i would have IBS
i bet my coffee would taste better
i'm certain his coffee tastes like gold
and success

he pulls out a bag of cheddar cheese
pretty people … they're just like us
i can't believe how good
that cheese must taste
in his perfectly symmetrical mouth
i bet it tastes like the cow that made it
won a beauty pageant
a cow that makes cheese that
ugly people can't eat

in a perfect world
i might have the guts to speak to him
no, in a *really* perfect world
he stares at me
muses for a moment and thinks
wow, look at that girl
she wears red plaid
like she invented it

laundry queen

i saw you while doing the laundry and thought
how is it even fair that anyone could look that beautiful doing laundry
like how is it actually fair
that i am a potato
and you are some much nicer looking type of vegetable
and i wanted to tell you
in a totally non creepy
girl to girl empowering supportive type of way
that you should totally do a photoshoot in the laundry room
because it would be a big hit on Instagram
all edgy and raw and cool
and somehow these lights
don't make you look washed out and jaundice-y like they do to me
but i didn't tell you because that would be really weird
and boundaries are a thing
and no one wants to talk while holding their own dirty underpants
but i hope all your laundry went well
and that you clean the lint out of the dryer

all money is always dirty

how strange it is
that the wealthy are so clean
crisp a-line trousers
white teeth sip strawberries in champagne
skin soft as an Hermès scarf
the veal is slaughtered on marble
served on porcelain
immaculate decay
edible flowers for garnish
the sound of water hitting crystal
without smudge or scratch
his hands intertwine with her french tips
i touch money often behind the register
leaves black on my fingers, yet
no dirt beneath his fingernails
jewellery that won't stain
i walk past bay windows
one Porsche one Escalade
his and hers sinks
his and hers towels
in a slick space
where no blood sticks
perfect and effortless
and utterly clean
how strange
how strange it is

hot professor

hot professor wears stylish jacket
hot professor assigns his own work
in the syllabus
but nobody minds, because he is hot professor

hot professor is aging
but everyone thinks that
salt-and-pepper is very becoming
on hot professor

hot professor talks about his wife
single female is disappointed
despite knowing that a rendezvous
with hot professor
would be an inappropriate use
of hot professor's power, still
everyone is allowed to fantasize

it's nice to find an excuse
to talk to hot professor
"i really liked this book,
it was so profound,"
hot professor smiles
hot professor enjoys
an astute observation

hot professor is
an ok teacher
and likely an average husband
hot professor knows
that he is hot professor
hot professor is a silver fox
such terms do not exist
for women, only for men
like hot professor

few remember
what they learned
in hot professor's class
only that the class is worth taking
to gaze at hot professor

the pink lady

good omens in the darkness
of an ending summer
past the crosswalk
humza was hungry and mentioned
at least four times that he wanted garlic bread
we marvelled that we saw
a secret meeting—two raccoons, two cats,
one skunk—
and back on the street
at some crummy intersection
where all the natural light is disrupted
by neon OPEN signs
and fluorescent messages that say
COFFEE HERE
it was ugly and we thought
the magic had passed
just two hungry idiots now at 11:50
going to Pizza Pizza for garlic bread
and that was when she appeared
emerging from a fever dream
black car heading east
she leaned out the window
head resting over the door
she smiled
intently smiled and made eye contact
like she'd known us for a long time
like we were old friends
the red sign above flashing KIT KAT
coloured her and the car's interior
all pink
the blonde in her hair now pink as well

the car rounded the corner
her head still sticking out
still staring like i was supposed to wave
we went inside
"did you see her? do you know her?"
and you described it too, you had no clue
who she was but even you said
it felt just like a dream

rules for everyone

the woman in the bright green satin
every glimmer every ripple
mesmerizes all the sunshine
caressing the silk
silver snakes dangle from her ears
hair up in a clip so
effortlessly beautiful
shines with every sway
but she and her boyfriend
walk so damn slow
and i can't move past
so i am obligated to hate them
even the pretty people
are not allowed to walk that slow
in the city

Chapter 7
Liminal Spaces

noun: **liminal space**
the aesthetic known as a liminal space is a location
which is a transition between two other locations or
states of being

gasoline

it is a rite of passage to mix every slushie flavour
into one sugary smorgasbord of ice cold slush
to pretend that Popeyes candy sticks
are cigarettes and that Rockets are ecstasy

we put air in our tires at the bicycle pump
we once liked the smell of gasoline
we thought oil slicks on the tarmac were beautiful

gas stations see more diversity
of human life
than places of worship
it's not a temple, but
purgatory
a place where you can buy Hostess Cupcakes
buy a life-changing lotto ticket
and destroy the planet at the same time

god made man
man made gas stations,
gas stations end man
and i bought Pepsi slushies there

SLUSHIES FOR BRAIN
FREEZE ENDURANCE
TESTING.

CIGARETTES
TO LOOK COOL.

CANCER IT LOOKS COOL

POWDERED SUGAR CANDY
(*redacted brand name*)
TO SIMULATE BLOW.

law and order: check-out counter

the clock is ticking
it's your turn to pay but
mum isn't back with onions
the groceries inch forward
every moment pure agony
how will you pay, you've got
nothing, if you hold up the line
the people will riot
the line between order and anarchy
is where the conveyor ends
and the scanner begins
the first beep rings
a piercing hollow sound
she's scanning the milk
she's scanning the apples
a whirlpool churns in your gut
the end is near
civilization heading for a collapse
your eyes scan the store
frantic you just want your mommy
she emerges, your beacon
your messiah, like christ
resurrected she appears from aisle two
onions in hand, the line parts for her
a miracle truly, your faith is restored
god is good. onions are good
and they are absolutely essential
to the recipe

mall rats

makeover at the mall
no money, mostly 14, but
let's go to the store for
19-year-old girls.
men want hotties in
hot-pink clubbing dress
ruching down the side
"great at hiding stomach rolls"
says sassy store clerk,
gold chains to accentuate
the boobies they don't have yet

smoothies at the food court
low fat no fat, 14-year-olds
can't get fat
collect free samples of
lotion, perfume, whatever
from overeager kiosk salesmen
wander into Claire's
these would look so hot
with that dress
that no one's mother would let them buy
pool change together
buy 3-way friendship bracelet
split the pics at the photo booth
oh my gosh, between
smoothie slurps,
the mall is the best
we'll be friends forever

waiting room at the edge of the cosmos

i wonder what he has

the repulsions of the human body
at the doctor's office, this waiting room
is a prison, this magazine is from 2008
this kid looks diseased, this mother
looks pissed, i'm diseased and i'm pissed
we're all sick and enraged in this
stuffy cage they call the doctor's office waiting room

everyone is getting called before me
and yet everyone is getting called before
everyone, because the doctor's office waiting room
is a time warp at the nexus of the universe

unbearable squirming, please god
i'm yearning to pee, they made me
drink a litre before getting here,
damn this ultrasound, damn this
receptionist, damn this bitch next to me
she got to go in first, don't they know
my kidneys are burning, damn
that man in the chair across
don't you fucking look at me we're all
gonna die in here

"sabrina? sabrina?" i'm not sabrina,
sabrina goes in, she was suffering too but
i'm suffering as well, we're all suffering
in the doctor's office waiting room

"excuse me excuse me" i'm pushing past
the people waiting to check in,
"please where's the bathroom"
"you can't pee before your ultrasound"
she says amid gum smacks
"i don't care, where's the bathroom"
she points with that bony painted finger
of hers i run to the bathroom there's a
waterfall coming out of me i don't care
about the ultrasound i'll condemn my body
to hell for one good piss

my name is called as soon as i exit the bathroom
are you fucking kidding me?

the salon

hairstylists often double as therapists
in between blow-dries and blowouts
talk of divorce and the way men fail
how they always, ultimately fail
how bleach will fry your hair and how
you could pull off that colour just go for it

i'm sure men's barbershops function
in the same way, get a fresh fade
a crisp line up and tell
your barber how women nag how
they always, ultimately nag
in between a shear and a shave
reassure yourself that highlights
are for manly men with big dicks too

at the salon, the longer you sit
the more you wanna talk you wanna
tell her about your hair texture and
how your job's been shit and your
mother-in-law is a real bitch
kids waiting on a bench bored
out of their mind during mommy's bob cut

some nine-year-old hauled to a chair
"it's time to get rid of that moustache sweetie"

stylists talk, salons sing
with the noise of scissors and dryers
and sinks, don't squirm sit still
put your head up and smile
this frames your face perfectly
who cares what he thinks
what the hell does he know
he's bald anyway

that one house

one house in every neighbourhood

bears a stain, for no reason sometimes,
it's just a gut instinct.
the kids say "that's the creepy house,
it's cursed."
you cross the street rather than
walking next to creepy house
especially at night
the blinds are often drawn
it has no personality but
a definitive presence.
in your neighbourhood it could be
home to some strange old hermit
or a somewhat-off childless couple

in my neighbourhood we had no clue
who dwelled within, different folks
would come and go
in my best friend's neighbourhood
it was a family with two violent sons
in dylan's old neighbourhood
it was the conspiracy nut next door
i remember when i crept up
the side of creepy house, peered
through the fence. mountains of
garbage bags in the yard
bodies we figured, what else?

ASPECTS OF A CREEPY HOUSE:

OMINOUS SILHOUETTE IN THE WINDOW

YOU WILL NEVER SEE THE INSIDE OF THE GARAGE.

SUSPICIOUS GARBAGE; I MEAN THIS ONE IS LITERALLY SHAPED LIKE A BODY.

WHAT KIND OF COLOUR CHOICE IS THIS?!

even now in this crummy high-rise
creepy house is creepy unit
(it's the man down the hall
plus dozens of others upstairs)
and if you're not sure
which house in your neck of the woods
is creepy house
it might be yours

the street you grew up on

meet at the mailbox
tag at dusk
sand in my shoes
nauseous on the swings
vandalize
underneath the slide
M+H = BFFS
alerted to the faint hum
of the ice cream truck
ride bikes and
abandoned shopping carts
down the hill
haul them back uphill
ring doorbells and run away
the thrill of small crimes
call landlines and say
"is so-and-so there?
can she come out and play?"
home before dark
mummy's cooked
chicken and rice
we'll meet at the mailbox tomorrow
and the day after too
until one day
we stop

"WELL, SHIT"

Chapter 8
Wizards and Crones

noun: **wizard**; plural noun: **wizards**
a man who has magical powers, especially in legends and fairy tales

noun: **crone**
in folklore, a crone is an old woman who may be characterized as disagreeable, malicious, or sinister in manner, often with magical or supernatural associations that can make her either helpful or obstructive

the collector

the collector forgoes a husband
for things; conjures images
of lonely spinsters
but you ought not to feel bad for her.
she dwells in a palace
of pearl and roses
serenades her birds with
classic Bollywood hits,
their sweet chirps
echo across marble.
the garden is a labyrinth
a castle of white flower towering
over such a small woman,
magnets and figurines
from Thailand to St. Petersburg,
the world is her oyster
her ocean, why choose marriage
or children?
it would only reduce her closet space.

everybody ages

there's a man in my building
who screams all day
he is old and probably very sick
screams bounce along the hallway
the sign of a normal day
this is a common circumstance
only silence is uncommon

if i told you that i felt only sympathy
at every one of his
moans, groans, screams, yelps
i would be a better person
and a liar

it is shameful but
i've caught myself feeling uncomfortable,
agitated, even angry
wishing he would quiet down
wishing he could form words
because the gibberish unnerves me
i quiet my selfishness
remind myself that he is very elderly
and very sick.
irritation melts into shame
and my shame warps into fear

who will hear me scream when the time comes?

the dichotomy of grannies

two types of old ladies exist on the bus.
one is wholesome granny
covered in pastel wool,
she knitted the scarf herself
and assures you it's easy to learn
you chat at the bus stop
complain about delays and snow,
she will be your surrogate grandmother
for the next half hour.
exchange pleasant smiles
over bumps and harsh brakes
each one jostling her tiny raisin-like frame.
she waves goodbye
at her stop, you have to stop yourself
from saying awww
because she's small and wrinkled
and lovely and you hope
you might be her one day

the second is
almost wholesome granny
a twinkle in her eye
and a big ol' vintage-looking grandma bag
jostling around her paper-thin lap,
a stylish beret atop cleanly parted grey hairs,
does she know her aesthetic is very *in* right now?
so you smile, for you trust
she seems nice enough,
until she says something
vaguely racist about the neighbourhood
and you spend the rest of the ride
awkwardly avoiding eye contact

poet

photos of his friends
and all have passed.
victims of the '80s,
cheeky smiles of leather boys
baby-faced but hard-bodied,
too young to die too gay
for the world to care.
the frames line a narrow hallway
before a cramped staircase
leading to shelves upon shelves
of occult text, volumes spilling
magic, divinity, simplicity, excess,
the collection is vast
not just books but
memories and ghosts.
i welcome the haunting
it is benevolent and necessary.
"this is why we need our elders,"
i tell him, he nods and we sip
earl grey mixed with english
breakfast, his special concoction,
discuss violent pasts
and uncertain futures.
i gaze in fascination
at records, vintage tins,
blankets, biscuits
and we agree
now it's up to us young ones,
our turn has come
to walk past death
and lead the way

a nana like mine

i looked at an old photo of my nana
her hair was jet black
tucked away, slick as elegant
oil-spill onyx
in a neat bun
her sari,
perfectly draped
modest and simple
perfect in its folds a
paper crane neatly
constructed
standing in all its delicate beauty
standing like
it could just blow away in the wind
but it doesn't

her hair was jet black
thick and smooth
not a night sky but
a black lake
deep steady
smelling like the horizon
air crisp
and damp

i looked at an old photo of my nana
her sari,
perfectly draped
she looked like a movie star
bigger than Audrey Hepburn more
classic more picturesque more
timeless more everything
perfect in folds
my nana is a paper crane
and i think to myself
i am a wrinkled clump of paper
i stand with my feet heavy
rooted deeply into the ground
my legs grow past sediment
and hers
look as if they are floating

what is it about these old pictures?
why do they always look perfect?
did my nana's hair always look
like god took ink and gently
smeared it on her head as a baby?
did my nana always stand
as if weightless as if
her life was easy when it wasn't?

i hope one day someone would look at my photos
i hope they see my curly black hair and think
they are twisted vines
wild, coarse, bouncing
with the beat of the city
i hope they see my jeans and think
she wears them so perfectly
what a special girl
a classic girl
a girl worth remembering

i know
i will never be a paper crane
the way nana is
but i will fold myself anyway
i will find an animal to be.

Acknowledgements

To the friends, family, and strangers who appear in this collection. Thank you for your humanity, your flaws, your brightness, your ugliness, and your beauty.

To my editor Shazia Hafiz Ramji, for her endless support and wisdom; to everyone at Book*hug Press for trusting my vision, honouring my words, and making this possible from the start.

PHOTO: BALI SINGH

About the Author

Hana Shafi is a writer and artist who illustrates under the name Frizz Kid. Both her visual art and writing frequently explore themes such as feminism, body politics, racism, and pop culture. She's published articles in publications such as *The Walrus*, *Hazlitt*, and *This Magazine* and has been featured on Buzzfeed, the CBC, *Flare*, and *Shameless*. She is also the recipient of the Women Who Inspire Award from the Canadian Council for Muslim Women in 2017. Her first book, *It Begins With The Body*, was selected by CBC Books as one of the best poetry books of 2018. Her second book, a compilation of essays and illustrations from her notable affirmation art series titled *Small, Broke, and Kind of Dirty: Affirmations for the Real World*, came out in 2020. Hana and her family immigrated to Mississauga from Dubai in 1996, and she now lives in Toronto with her two cute, but sometimes annoying, cats.

Colophon

Manufactured as the first edition of
People You Know, Places You've Been
in the fall of 2023 by Book*hug Press

Edited for the press by Shazia Hafiz Ramji
Copy edited by Andrea Waters
Proofread by Charlene Chow
Design and typesetting by Gareth Lind, Lind Design
Typeset in Macklin and Verveine

Printed in Canada

bookhugpress.ca